EAT LIKE
A LOCAL-
NASHVILLE

Nashville Tennessee Food Guide

Tim Fedorko

CZYK Publishing Since 2011.
CZYKPublishing.com
Eat Like a Local

Lock Haven, PA
All rights reserved.
ISBN: 9798713733018

BOOK DESCRIPTION

Are you excited about planning your next trip? Do you want an edible experience? Would you like some culinary guidance from a local? If you answered yes to any of these questions, then this Eat Like a Local book is for you. Eat Like a Local - Nashville by Tim Fedorko. Tim Fedorko shares the best local dining experiences in Nashville. Culinary tourism is an important aspect of any travel experience. Food has the ability to tell you a story of a destination, its landscapes, and culture on a single plate. Most food guides tell you how to eat like a tourist. Although there is nothing wrong with that, as part of the Eat Like a Local series, this book will give you a food guide from someone who has lived at your next culinary destination.

In these pages, you will discover advice on having a unique edible experience. This book will not tell you exact addresses or hours but instead will give you excitement and knowledge of food and drinks from a local that you may not find in other travel food guides.

Eat like a local. Slow down, stay in one place, and get to know the food, people, and culture. By the time you finish this book, you will be eager and prepared to travel to your next culinary destination.

OUR STORY

Traveling has always been a passion of the creator of the Eat Like a Local book series. During Lisa's travels in Malta, instead of tasting what the city offered, she ate at a large fast-food chain. However, she realized that her traveling experience would have been more fulfilling if she had experienced the best of local cuisines. Most would agree that food is one of the most important aspects of a culture. Through her travels, Lisa learned how much locals had to share with tourists, especially about food. Lisa created the Eat Like a Local book series to help connect people with locals which she discovered is a topic that locals are very passionate about sharing. So please join me and: Eat, drink, and explore like a local.

TABLE OF CONTENTS

11. Frothy Monkey is About Much More Than Good Coffee

12. Devour a Donut (or Two) From Donut Distillery

13. Fall in Love with Biscuits at Biscuit Love

14. McDougal's Chicken Fingers & Wings Defines What a Chicken Finger Is Supposed to Taste Like

15. Southern BBQ and Great Vibes at Martin's Bar-B-Que Joint

16. Make Your Own Smores at Caney Fork Restaurant

17. The Picnic Tap is the Spot for a Brew and a Dog

18. Taste and Experience Mediterranean Cuisine at Lyra

19. Country Cuisine Done Right at Arnold's Country Kitchen

20. The Speakeasy at Hotel Noelle is Worth Talking About

21. Nashville's Little Italy is Coco's Italian Market

22. Rolf and Daughters is the Spot for Communal Dishes and Cocktails

23. Nashville's Best Thai at Bangkokville Thai Cuisine

24. Midnight Breakfast at Monell's

25. You'll Be Too Full to Walk Out of Peg Leg Porker

26. Comfort Food and Moon Shine at The Stillery

READ OTHER BOOKS BY

CZYK PUBLISHING

DEDICATION

This book is dedicated to Cheech & Ares. The first of many to be dedicated to the little furballs. It is also dedicated to my parents, whose love of travel and food introduced me to what would become an unwavering passion of mine.

ABOUT THE AUTHOR

Tim Fedorko is an accomplished chef and entrepreneur. He has owned and operated several food concepts in his home state of Florida. He currently lives in Nashville where he is a hospitality consultant, freelance writer, and a food author. He resides in East Nashville, within walking distance of many of the great places chosen for this list.

HOW TO USE THIS BOOK

The goal of this book is to help culinary travelers either dream or experience different edible experiences by providing opinions from a local. The author has made suggestions based on their own knowledge. Please do your own research before traveling to the area in case the suggested locations are unavailable.

Travel Advisories: As a first step in planning any trip abroad, check the Travel Advisories for your intended destination.
https://travel.state.gov/content/travel/en/traveladvisories/traveladvisories.html

FROM THE PUBLISHER

Traveling can be one of the most important parts of a person's life. The anticipation and memories that you have are some of the best. As a publisher of the *Eat Like a Local*, Greater Than a Tourist, as well as the popular *50 Things to Know* book series, we strive to help you learn about new places, spark your imagination, and inspire you. Wherever you are and whatever you do I wish you safe, fun, and inspiring travel.

Lisa Rusczyk Ed. D.
CZYK Publishing

Great food isn't just about taste.
It is also about texture, appearance,
aroma, and most importantly; great
food is about the experience it
creates.

- Chef Tim Fedorko

I am both a chef and foodie. The two often go hand in hand but in truth not all chefs are foodies, and most foodies are not chefs. The difference to me is that foodies just want to eat good food. We may not care about who made it, or why. We just want something made with care and that can provide an experience. I have always had a passion for eating. My family background is diverse and allowed me to enjoy many cuisines growing up. We love to eat and talk, and I have found over the years that if the conversation is dry and mundane, then you are eating a meal. When the conversation is lively, energetic, and engaging then that means you are having an experience. The chatter may not be about the food, but good food and hospitality is an artform that promotes good conversation.

Traveling is another passion of mine. For me, traveling and experiencing food go hand in hand. Some people travel like they are window shopping, trying to hit as many places as possible. There is nothing wrong with that, it's just not my style. I would rather spend a few days in the same city. That way you get to know how the people eat, not the tourists. The reception you get after frequenting the same coffee shop a few days in a row is different. You develop relationships. You start to have experiences. This is my way to find out where the locals eat. This collection of 50 tips to eat like a local in Nashville can help you experience the city the way a local foodie would.

Nashville
Tennessee, USA

Nashville Tennessee Climate

	High	Low
January	47	29
February	52	32
March	62	40
April	71	48
May	79	57
June	87	65
July	90	70
August	89	68
September	83	62
October	72	49
November	61	40
December	51	32

GreaterThanaTourist.com

Temperatures are in Fahrenheit degrees.
Source: NOAA

1. SIP AN ESPRESSO AND ENJOY A PARISIAN SANDWICH AT CITIZEN MARKET

Let's just get this out of the way now. I grew up in South Florida and have espresso running through my blood. The whole caffeine part is cool and all but for me it's about the flavor and aroma. I don't add anything to my espresso. Anyone can say coffee is good if it's loaded with sugar and syrup, and I'm not knocking you if that's your style. I'm just a purist who will gladly walk an extra twenty minutes for the right roast. Enter, Citizen Market.

Citizen Market is one of the three incredible food stalls at Hunters Station that I mention in this list (although everything there is pretty solid.). Hunter's Station is over a mile from where I live, and I still trek down there several times a week. Citizen Market offers a collection of craft foods sourced by small local producers and they are very particular about their products. I've enjoyed every single thing I've tried, most of which coming from completely different producers.

My usual go to is an espresso and one of these little French style chocolate cakes that was probably made in heaven. When I'm looking for a quick and satisfying lunch, I also pick up a Parisian Sandwich. It's baked ham, salted butter, and creamy brie layered on a fresh baked baguette (ask them to heat it up a bit). I also recommend the homemade pop-tarts.

2. EXPERIENCE SOUTHERN AND MIDDLE EASTERN FUSION AT BUTCHER & BEE

The first thing to note about Butcher & Bee in East Nashville is that from the outside you only see a relatively plain brick wall. The inside of the restaurant is beautiful, but it is dwarfed by how incredibly gorgeous and relaxing their patio area is. Ask to sit out there, even if it's cold. They have heaters and the ambience at night is enchanting.

Now let's talk about the menu. Fusion food can be risky and my first thought when I saw Middle Eastern and Southern fusion was to be skeptically excited. I ordered their 5-course chef's tasting option, which is usually what I do when I try new places that offer a tasting menu. Everything I ate was incredible and a clever blend of the two cuisines. I've been back more times than I can recall. If you have a pretty open mind towards food, I recommend going with the tasting. Then let the server pair wine for you and sit back and enjoy the vibes. They have a great selection of local wines, beers, and even spirits.

3. DRINK WITH THE LOCALS AT EAST NASHVILLE BEER WORKS

There are a lot of great breweries in Nashville, but East Nashville Beer Works stands out. They have a phenomenal selection of beers and are frequently introducing something new. Yet, despite the quantity approach, they've not compromised on quality. The food options are also consistently good and served generously. My favorite beer is their Miro Miel. It's a honey blonde ale that pairs well with anything. It's just light enough not to fill you up but still full of flavor and aroma.

On top of the great beer and food selection, East Nashville Beer Works is known as one of the most family friendly breweries in town and has one of my favorite patios. You can even bring your four-legged friends into the beer garden. They do get very busy on the weekends, so I tend to visit weeknights. It's a more local crowd those nights as well.

4. TACOS AURORA IS THE SPOT FOR TACO TUESDAY

Taco's Aurora is another one of the food stalls inside Hunters Station that I frequent multiple times a week. Of course, Taco Tuesday is the best day to get a deal but sometimes the hankering for good tacos doesn't care what day it is. They also get slammed on Tuesdays.

When I was in line the first time, I heard something I don't hear very often in Nashville, Spanish. I grew up in South Florida and hearing other languages, especially Spanish, is a reminder of home. I don't know why hearing the crew at Taco's Aurora talking gave me an intuitive feeling that the food was going to be good, but it did.

My intuition was not wrong. I've tried every taco they have, even their vegan options. All of them were well crafted and delicious. Hands down the best taco's in Nashville in my opinion. I recommend their barbacoa and nopal corn salad tacos (yes, corn salad. Just try it.).

5. MITCHELL DELI IS A NY STYLE DELI IN THE HEART OF NASHVILLE

My mother is Jewish and in South Florida there is a large Jewish population, most of which originally hailed from the northeast coast. In cities like Miami and New York it is really easy to find a good deli. In many other cities it can take time to find the winner. Every city should have a traditional NY-style deli and no offense to those corporate NY themed deli establishments, but they wouldn't know a smear if it got smeared on their face.

It takes time to make good deli food. Yes, soups and sandwiches seem simple enough but if you have ever tried to make your own chicken soup or your own pastrami, you know there is a difference between expertly developed flavor and opening a package of vacuum sealed deli meat. A good deli understands that a bone broth and quality corned beef is just the tip, or the crust if you will.

Mitchell Deli, in my humble opinion, could easily hold its own against some of the NY deli titans. (I am going to spend more time calming down my friends from NY after this gets published then it takes to make a proper pastrami. Which if you are curious is never less then 3 days. Uh-huh, days.) Mitchell Deli gets it. Their soups and deli meats are top notch, and they understand the details. Just the right amount of mustard, fresh rye bread cut just at the ideal thickness, pickles that took as long to make as the meats.

Whether you want a Rueben, a simple smoked turkey and swiss, a fresh bagel, or a cup of soup that is teeming with love and comfort, Mitchell Deli will have you saying, 'Mazltov!".

6. YEAST NASHVILLE IS THE HOME FOR KOLACHES

I had no idea what a Kolache was when I first visited Yeast Nashville. I discovered it during my journey to compare all the espresso options within walking distance and I also wanted to check out their bakery options. Walking up to Yeast Nashville one early morning I was greeted by a very long line. If this happens, don't be discouraged. Your patience will be rewarded. I view long lines at eateries as a great omen.

A kolache is a baked good from the hand pie family. There is nothing not to love about those two words together. Yeast Nashville has sweet and savory options for their kolaches. These options rotate but one of their staple savory options is the sausage and cheese kolache. That one is my go-to. They source the sausage locally and use a sharp cheddar that melts just enough and doesn't overpower the sausage. It is basically an elevated pig in a blanket (a set of words that I think you'd agree has less allure than "hand pie.").

As far as the sweet kolaches go, every option I have tried was incredible, but my favorite sweet at Yeast Nashville is their cinnamon roll. Ask for it warm. Order two. If you still want a data point on which sweet kolache to get, my family all favor the apple cinnamon option. Oh, and in case you are wondering, they have great coffee. They are my one of my favorite espressos within walking distance of my apartment. Not that I have a detailed excel spread sheet with map links and notes or anything.

7. EXPERIENCE CULINARY CRAFTMANSHIP AT THE CHEF & I

Oh, the Chef & I. If I could afford to eat here every day I would. A small comfortable space with table dining, a bar, and for me the only place to sit - with the chefs. You can kind of imagine the setup as similar to a Hibachi place. The difference is that instead of a show of twirling eggs and onion volcanos, you get to watch artists at work.

If you want, you can order off of the menu. I'm not sure what is on the menu because I've never looked at it. When you walk in you see a chalkboard that has their 5 and 7 course offerings. It's not in great detail, usually just simple words like Quail, Shrimp Ceviche, etc. Nothing that gives you any idea of what they did with the quail, or how they will serve the shrimp ceviche.

I view it as a "when in Rome" situation. This isn't line cooks executing under a chef's direction, this is the chefs executing under their own direction. The chef's there are given freedom to change and reinterpret the menu the way they see fit. Thus, I don't care about the menu, I want the items written in chalk that a fellow Chef was inspired to make that day. You can never go wrong when you eat food made with passion.

8. EUROPEAN ELEGANCE AT THE BARISTA PARLOR

Barista Parlor is another coffee shop I've discovered in my city-wide espresso hunt. They have a few locations in Nashville but all of them have the same stark, modern, European style décor. A décor that I have always enjoyed in coffee shops. Their Germantown location has the coffee bar in the middle and is surrounded by seating. The counter is spacious, void of clutter, and highlights to quality of their equipment. It offers a kind of Zen feel.

They also had a few options of fresh baked goods, all of which had a European flair. I felt transported back to coffee shops I'd visited in Spain and France. It's a different type of comfortable elegance that can be hard to explain. You'll just have to go check it out yourself.

9. THE JOY OF JOYLAND

Joyland is what you get when you get take a well-known local chef and tell them to make a place that sells comfort food. In this case, it's southern style comfort food. Specifically, its burgers, shakes, biscuits, southern fried chicken, and a few sides. That's it. Nothing too fancy, just flawlessly executed.

Joyland takes a from-scratch approach to recreate southern classics made with a chef's expertise. They also have pretty good coffee, and pretty darn good chocolate hand pies. I usually get a biscuit sandwich but have also gone with the burger a few times. It's the kind of menu where you don't have to worry about branching out.

10. THE SECRET IS OUT ABOUT BLACK DYNASTY RAMEN

Good ramen is tricky business. The individual ingredients are critical. Whether you opt for pork belly, tofu, or chicken thighs, the manner in which those ingredients are crafted and then delicately placed on top of the ramen noodles is what most people identify as the make or break for a good bowl of ramen. I can feel my fellow ramen fiends shaking their heads as they read that. Yes, the ingredients are important, as are the noodles (which I'm fairly certain Black Dynasty makes from scratch), but none of it matters if there isn't a deep, rich broth to marry them all together.

Unlike soups and stews, the ingredients in Ramen are added to the broth at the last minute. They won't be simmered slowly for hours allowing them to bring their flavors to the party. A ramen broth has to immediately take a bunch of standalone ingredients and make them become instant bed partners. Without broth, ramen is just a bunch of stuff in a bowl. Even if it is delicious stuff.

Black Dynasty Ramen features three different broths. They have a vegan one with hints of green onion and savory mushroom, a clear chicken broth, and my favorite, what they describe as a creamy pork broth. I would guess that the creaminess comes from bone marrow. This broth is out of this world rich. Like Egyptian pharaoh rich. The silky fatty delicious oil clings to the sides of your mouth as you slurp it down.

The kicker about Black Dynasty Ramen is that it is supposed to be a secret. When they first hit the scene, they were a pop-up and the only way to find them was to follow their Instagram. Now that the secret is out, just head downtown and go to Bar Sovereign. Walk to the back alley, just follow your nose, you'll understand why they didn't stay a secret for long.

11. FROTHY MONKEY IS ABOUT MUCH MORE THAN GOOD COFFEE

I originally stumbled across Frothy Monkey one evening looking for an espresso (this shouldn't surprise you at this point). Most of the really good coffee houses aren't open late and I typically like to have coffee after dinner. There are a few Frothy Monkey locations in Nashville, and I've been to all of them at this point.

Right when I walked in, I could see why they were still open. They start at coffee and baked goods and go all the way to wine, cheese, and French-American inspired entrees. All of which are available most of the day. Many places that have such a variety of options aren't able to execute them all properly. Frothy Monkey does.

It is possible to spend an entire day at Frothy Monkey. I've done it. You start with coffee and a danish. Move to another coffee and one of their lunch offerings. Then end the night with a glass of wine and their cheese and charcuterie plate. If you're me, you also have another coffee.

12. DEVOUR A DONUT (OR TWO) FROM DONUT DISTILLERY

The Donut Distillery is one of two donut places that made this list. You may find this odd, considering my outspoken love for bakery sweets, but I am not the biggest donut fan. Nothing against them, I'd just rather a danish than a donut. (I am going to spell it right just once, so I feel better, doughnut, ok I'm good now.) The exception to that preference is when a place specializes in donuts. I mean they literally distill them here. I'm not sure if I will be able to make that work or not, let's see.

Donut Distillery takes its specialization seriously. They make donuts, that's it. Just really freaking good ones, that also happen to be mini donuts. Which depending on how you view things means that they really don't count as cheating. The menu is full of custom donuts created by the Donut Distillery and also allows you to customize your own decadent desires. Oh yeh, they also have a donut milkshake, which you can get with or without alcohol.

That's right I made it happen! The distillery part has nothing to do with the donuts. It has to do with the only other thing on Donut Distillery's menu – booze. Not just any booze, Donut Distillery offers a small but select wine menu, a variety of local brews, as well as spirits. You can have a shot of tequila and a donut and no one will judge you even slightly. They even have a portion of the menu devoted to pairing their custom donuts with their beer and mimosa selections.

13. FALL IN LOVE WITH BISCUITS AT BISCUIT LOVE

If you've ever made biscuits, then you know that sometimes even with so few ingredients, things go wrong. They're more a labor of love then recipe you just follow. Biscuit Love was aptly named. Their biscuits are incredibly fresh and flavorful. Just the right amount of butter and salt. It's clear they make them fresh.

But it doesn't stop there. You could go with just biscuits and gravy (I'll never knock the classics), but for me I always go with the East Nasty. It's one of their homemade biscuits stuffed with a fried chicken thigh, aged cheddar, and their sausage gravy. They source the sausage locally and the batter on the fried chicken has just the right amount of heat to really get your tastebuds working.

If you still have room, or you're like me and will always make room for sweets, you have to try the B Roll. Think biscuit falls in love with cinnamon roll. You'll find room.

41

14. MCDOUGAL'S CHICKEN FINGERS & WINGS DEFINES WHAT A CHICKEN FINGER IS SUPPOSED TO TASTE LIKE

I tend to judge places on how well they execute simple dishes. Chicken Fingers are a simple classic that can either be satisfying because they hit that familiar craving button, or they can be superbly satisfying because they didn't just come out of the freezer. Let's face it, even the frozen ones can be good if you've got a hankering. Now, if you have chicken fingers in your name, they better be superbly satisfying.

McDougal's said, "challenge accepted." It was actually probably, "Hold my beer.", because they have a great selection of local beers on tap. But back to the finger licking, delicately fried, perfectly seasoned chicken fingers; which are on point. I'm a honey mustard guy but they also have some killer hot sauce options. I haven't had their wings yet, but I can only assume they earn the right to be a part of McDougal's name as well.

15. SOUTHERN BBQ AND GREAT VIBES AT MARTIN'S BAR-B-QUE JOINT

Martin's Bar-B-Que Joint has a few locations in Tennessee. I frequent their Downtown Nashville location. The vibe of the restaurant is everything you want from a BBQ Joint. Each table has an assortment of homemade BBQ sauces in plain squeeze bottles next to a napkin dispenser. You'll need those.

Martin's Bar-B-Que Joint hits a homerun with all the meats on their menu. You really can't go wrong. Trust me I've tested this theory over and over. And over. My dad grew up in Texas and likes to be particularly harsh on brisket made outside of the longhorn state. He has been unable to provide any criticism on account of having his mouth full. I don't blame him. The brisket is my favorite option at Martin's. It's about the crust, and the smoke ring, and the tenderness, and the spices, and the smokey flavor, oh the smokey flavor.

Now there is a lot of great BBQ in Nashville, but what separates Martin's from the pack in my opinion is that they paid just as much attention to their sides and ambience as they did to their proteins. My little brother usually just orders a giant serving of mac-n-cheese and then picks off pieces of pulled pork when my dad gets distracted by all the cool memorabilia hanging on the walls. I don't blame him, the place is pretty cool, and the downtown location opens up to this beautiful courtyard. Great for relaxing naps between plates.

16. MAKE YOUR OWN SMORES AT CANEY FORK RESTAURANT

I will admit, Caney Fork probably doesn't get a lot of local traffic. But that just means some locals are missing out. There are two things about Caney Fork that I make the trip for: the wild game options and the make your own s'mores dessert.

I'm the type of eater who will try anything twice. If that is a mantra you can get behind than I recommend you try the wild game platter. We are talking frog legs, gator tail, quail, and other less common meats. All of it prepared southern style.

Round off the evening with their s'more's dessert. They bring out the essentials and a small 'campfire'. Everyone knows exactly how they like their marshmallow and it's fun to play with fire indoors.

17. THE PICNIC TAP IS THE SPOT FOR A BREW AND A DOG

The Picnic Tap is one of a few of the great food stalls inside Hunters Station in East Nashville. I like to take a daily walk which I claim is for my health, but it really just helps me validate eating again. Sometimes I'll take a lunch break from writing and make my way down Main Street to Hunters Station for a hot dog and a cold beer (it helps the creativity).

As a chef I appreciate two types of food the most. On one hand, I love high-level culinary craftmanship. On the other hand, there is nothing like a classic dish done right. The Picnic Tap sources its dogs and buns from local artisans and you can taste the quality with your first bite. I keep it simple, plain dog with a side of stone-ground mustard. They even grill the bun a little. Who doesn't like a nice warm bun?

18. TASTE AND EXPERIENCE MEDITERRANEAN CUISINE AT LYRA

Here in the states, Mediterranean cuisine is delivered in one of two ways. Either you're grabbing a gyro from a quick service restaurant or you're sitting down to an elegant meal. Lyra is the place to go for that elegant meal. The Mediterranean diet is woven into the fabric of the Mediterranean lifestyle. This is a region of the world that cherishes the experience of eating as much as what they are eating. Dining at Lyra is the best way to enjoy this experience without stepping foot on a plane.

The menu at Lyra is supported by the ambience and quality of service in a manner that manifests into an experience. The menu fluctuates based on the seasonality of the ingredients Lyra sources. They also have fantastic specials. The last time I ordered Lyra they were offering a dish called Lambchetta. It was lamb stuffed with apricot and then slow roasted, served on top of roasted sweet potatoes with just the right amount of spice to balance the sweetness of the apricot. The dish was rounded out with an egg yolk that melded with the spice, creating a delicate and creamy sauce that brought the whole dish together. I have been stalking their social media in anticipation of the next time they offer it.

My last thoughts on dining at Lyra are to encourage you to submit to the experience. Make it a date night or dine with good friends. Don't rush through the meal. Throw away conventional American dining ideals by ordering a course at a time. Order wine, talk, relax, and enjoy the experience that Lyra has to offer. A group of my close friends and I used to have a ritual at certain restaurants. We all put our phones in the middle of the table and the first person to grab their phone paid the tab. Just food for thought.

19. COUNTRY CUISINE DONE RIGHT AT ARNOLD'S COUNTRY KITCHEN

Growing up in South Florida, my only introduction to country cuisine was on road trips when we would stop at a place that keeps its crackers in a barrel. I would be lying if I were to claim I still don't stop there on road trips, and I would also be lying if I were to say my appreciation for the comfort of country cuisine wasn't born of this chain. At the very least it provided me an introduction to a cuisine I have come to love. I would also argue that country cuisine is probably the strongest culinary import from the U.S. Although it hasn't yet been as proliferated as the hamburger. My apologies, Asia.

As my awareness of country cooking grew past the confines of the place with rocking chairs out front, I quickly realized there was much more to the cuisine then loads of butter and deep fried everything. Zero complaints about loads of butter or deep fried everything but it is much more difficult to make a baked chicken taste good then it is to batter it and deep fry it. I challenge you to find someone who will eat escargot without butter, garlic, and salt. That being said, country cuisine is very much about pleasing the gut.

Arnold's Country Kitchen is hailed by many as a Nashville institution. They have been serving up country and soul food dishes for over three decades. Dining there is a no-frills experience, as it should be. The food is served cafeteria style. You take what you want and as much of it as you want. The plates are white. The silverware basic. The napkins, paper. The food is the star, and oh boy does it shine. How many country restaurants do you know with a James Beard award?

The menu at Arnold's varies by the day. You can check it out on their website. My favorite country dish is country fried steak, so you'll likely find me there on Thursdays. There is just something magical about a crunchy and salty fried steak smothered in creamy and peppery gravy. Arnold's is only open from 10:30 to 2:45pm, which is just early enough that you can take a solid nap afterwards and still have some day left to eat again.

20. THE SPEAKEASY AT HOTEL NOELLE IS WORTH TALKING ABOUT

Hotel Noelle is an upscale, boutique hotel in downtown Nashville. I have not stayed there before but have friends who have, and they raved about it. Hotel Noelle offers more than just lodging. They have a few popular dining options. There restaurant is top notch, and they have a coffee shop that is also on this list. More on that later. Right now, I want to speak about the speakeasy (does that count as a Dad joke?). The hotel simply refers to it as a hidden bar and I will admit the first time I tried to find it (I was being stubborn and didn't want to ask for directions) it is pretty well hidden. I will help you out, the bar is underneath the hotel. No digging required.

The unique and secretive nature of Hotel Noelle's hidden bar is only part of its allure. You are awarded for your diligence by gaining access to a creative and eclectic cocktail menu. The icing on this mysterious cake is how well the food menu pairs with the drinks. The mixologist and chef had to have worked hand-in-hand to have developed such culinary cocktail cohesion (maybe they forgot how to get out and just live down there). I should say that they continue to work hand-in-hand because both times that I have ventured down past the storage room I have encountered a completely different menu (more proof that they are lost down there). That's right, I said storage room. Consider that your other free hint.

21. NASHVILLE'S LITTLE ITALY IS COCO'S ITALIAN MARKET

My parents, who live about an hour from Nashville, had caught wind of Coco's Italian Market from some friends of theirs. Our ritual when they come to visit me is to check out a new place every time. I think my Dad sent me a text every morning during the week leading up their next visit. All the text said was, "Leave the gun, take the cannoli.".

As you can imagine, we ate a few cannoli. (If you are going to look up the plural of cannoli now, I can save you some time and tell you I found nothing conclusive during my twenty second internet search).

We also stuffed our faces with other traditional Italian fare. My favorite was a ravioli dish with mushrooms and pancetta. I was very reluctant to share once I tasted it, but my Dad offered me something I couldn't refuse. We started with an antipasti plate featuring some wonderful, imported cheeses and meats (a way better dish when served cold compared to some revenge.). I would recommend starting there if it is your first time at Coco's.

After you're done eating you can load up on imported Italian goods from their market. They have a great selection of wine and olive oils. We also got more cannoli. My brother picked up a few pounds of Italian cookies and I of course grabbed a bag of Italian espresso beans. Everything on the menu is available to-go and some items are even already placed in aluminum containers, a great option for an easy dinner.

22. ROLF AND DAUGHTERS IS THE SPOT FOR COMMUNAL DISHES AND COCKTAILS

Rolf and Daughters is located in Germantown and honestly one of my favorite options for dining with a group of friends. Rolf and Daughters menu and atmosphere is clearly intended to be communal. The restaurant is located in an historic factory. The brick elements and openness of the space make you feel like you could be in an old factory cafeteria. Except this cafeteria has an incredible wine list, one which features mostly natural wines, and makes its own pasta.

The menu at Rolf & Daughters is a seasonal and creative approach to Italian. The menu is constantly evolving and highlights local produce elegantly. As I mentioned, this menu (this whole place really) is designed to invoke a sense of community. The dining room is set up with long rows of tables and it is inevitable that you will end up talking to the people next to you, whether you know them or not. This is a great place to go and mingle with the locals.

23. NASHVILLE'S BEST THAI AT BANGKOKVILLE THAI CUISINE

There is a short list of restaurant types that a true foodie city will include along with its locally inspired concepts. You know what I am talking about here. One of the best things about living in today's world is the variety of cuisines available. This means that everyone has a go-to "hole in the wall" place to go for Italian, Mexican, Chinese, Indian, and Thai. There are other foodie city staples of course, but as far as the international pantheon goes, I think those five are the obligatory cuisine types that should be a part of a foodie city's myriad of options.

Bangkokville was rumored to be the undeniable Thai titan here in Nashville. I have since confirmed this and will even go as far as to say Bangkokville is one of the best Thai places I've tried in the States.

Walking in to Bangkokville, you will immediately observe all the quality Thai staples. It's the little things, like a white linen tablecloth under a piece of glass, water served in red wine glasses, carrot flowers and other herbs garnishing even the simplest of dishes. I think even my side of white rice was adorned by a carrot flower. There are also the familiar smells, the air is filled with the aroma of garlic, ginger, fish sauce, and Thai chili. The menu is also in line with what one would expect from a Thai place.

Then there are the things that differentiate Bangkokville, the quality of the food. You can tell that they don't use as many frozen or pre-made products as some Thai restaurants. There peanut satay sauce was definitely homemade and to their credit I think they even made the effort to doctor up their Thai Chili Sauce. For those not in the restaurant industry here is a little secret, shortly after Siracha became the hipster ketchup, a type of Thai Chili Sauce known as Mae Ploy emerged on the scene and began appearing at every type of restaurant, from wing spot to steak house.

Most places just pour it from the bottle and call it Thai chili sauce, but sometimes restaurants add a little rice vinegar or fresh garlic to upgrade this incredibly versatile sauce. If I am correct that Bangkokville is one of these places, it only supports my notion that they really care about what they are putting on their plates (which of course, are the exact same ones you find at almost every other Thai place.). Don't fix what isn't broken, but never settle for ordinary when a little extra attention to detail can set you apart. My go-to at Bangkokville is their Thai Basil. Friendly reminder, I would start with a lower spice level and just ask for the spice tray. Control your own destiny.

24. MIDNIGHT BREAKFAST AT MONELL'S

I was first introduced to the Southern version of a French style course meal when I was in my teens traveling with my parents in Georgia. We stayed at a property in the mountains that had a main lodge and rented out cabins. We always stayed in the cabins but went to the lodge's dining hall sometimes for all three meals a day. One would think that after a week of that you'd get bored of the options. Nope. That lodge served meals the same way that Monell's does.

Every day is a different menu. You don't look at the menu unless you want to see what's going to be hitting your table. You order your drinks and sit down, then the food starts arriving family-style on big plates. When something is finished, they bring another round. The food is all traditional Southern of course, but with enough variety that you won't get bored. It's usually two meats and at least three sides (or fixins) and of course plenty of biscuits, cornbread, apple butter, and homemade jams. I recently learned that they now offer their perfectly crunchy and tender fried chicken with every meal.

Monell's has three locations in Nashville and I've heard they all have the same style and southern charm. The location I visited was their original location in Germantown, which looks like you would expect a Southern boarding house style restaurant to look (beautiful brick with a homely feel). Monell's serves breakfast, lunch, and dinner. They also have a midnight breakfast on Saturdays. It goes from midnight to 3am and you'd be surprised the type of crowd you'll see at the time. Totally worth staying up/waking up early for. The time I went I woke up early, went and stuffed my face, and then went back to bed. Slept like a very full baby.

25. YOU'LL BE TOO FULL TO WALK OUT OF PEG LEG PORKER

I'm pretty confident you can guess the cuisine featured at Peg Leg Porker. Yep, its BBQ. But Peg Leg Porker also understands that whole specialization thing. They have a few other proteins, a sausage, some chicken wings, and a chicken salad, but their main offerings are pork. Pulled pork, pork ribs, and pork rinds. Walking into Peg Leg Porker you are instantly hit by the aroma of smokey, savory, meaty deliciousness. This is another one of those no-frills type of places. The menu is an old school light up board with the little black letters positioned on it like scrabble pieces. Adding to charm is the plethora of printed out pieces of paper taped around the menu. Good old fashioned simple dining.

There are little bits of humor sprinkled into the menu and signage, something I have found to be quite unique to this type of eatery. It's just good ol' Southern charm. Instead of just writing "banana pudding" they wrote "Yes! We do have banana pudding.". And yes, that banana pudding was incredible. They also had Brunswick Stew that day.

Honestly, one of best cups of Brunswick Stew I have had (the hate mail is just building with these claims…I think I'll get a PO Box.). If they're offering the stew when you visit, just take some home. You will be too full of everything else. Another fun menu item that I recommend trying was their Kool-Aid pickles. Sounds odd, but the sweetness somehow really worked.

26. COMFORT FOOD AND MOON SHINE AT THE STILLERY

Growing up in South Florida, I didn't hear about moonshine until it came up in one of my high school history books. During prohibition moonshine was a cash cow for the mob and I also recall a passage talking about how "white lightning" was known to cause blindness. I had already tried absinthe at that point and had an idea that these super strong spirits didn't necessarily warrant their rep. Nonetheless, I didn't think moon shine was going to have the unique flavor profile that absinthe has. My best guess was that it would taste like the high proof grain alcohol that commonly finds its way into college "punch" bowls.

Well, I was wrong, and I owe that realization to The Stillery. They have a great selection of moonshine, which you can order neat or try in their cocktails. I typically avoid cocktails as I like to enjoy the subtleties of spirits on their own. I was hesitant about moonshine (see above), not because it may make me blind (ask my friends about my risk aversion…it's not a thing), but because I didn't want to take a shot of rubbing alcohol. I tried several of the shines featured at The Stillery, and while not my favorite spirit, I can see the appeal.

Oh, and the food, thank goodness for the food. Shine is still a strong spirit. I wasn't going blind, but if it wasn't for their warm and savory house-made pretzels or their baked cheese appetizer served with this incredible pesto bread, I may have been seeing in circles. They also feature wood-oven pizzas. I had the brussel sprouts pie. It came with roasted brussels, bacon, caramelized onions, and parmesan cheese. The perfect greasy and meaty tool to help offset the shine.

27. EAST PARK DONUT'S & COFFEE KNOWS CLASSIC DONUTS LIKE NO OTHER

East Park Donut's & Coffee is across the street from my apartment in East Nashville and was the first place I visited when I moved to the city. I have two to three espressos a day (I have a problem and I will be the first to admit it) and so I was well known at East Park pretty quick. Not only because it was close, but because they take their coffee and donuts seriously.

When you first walk in you are greeted by a display of their daily offerings. This usually consists of at least two dozen different donuts. They make everything from scratch and have a variety of donut types. You can keep it classic and opt for a glazed sour cream donut or get fancy with one of their craft selections.

If you happen to stop by during the weekend, then you can get one of their cinnamon rolls. Easily one of the best cinnamon rolls I have ever had (top 10 at least…and I have had a lot of cinnamon rolls). They also have allergen friendly and vegan donut options as well as a full menu of other items. They make a killer oatmeal for those chilly mornings and they open up nice and early.

28. THERE IS PLENTY TO LOVE AT LOVELESS CAFE

There is a lot to love about Loveless Café. If I am being honest the name makes no sense, because this is Southern food with its most important ingredient, love. Located in West Nashville, Loveless Café is one of a few country style kitchens that made this list. Just like the other ones, I recommend sweatpants. That is not a jab at the casual vibe offered by Loveless, it is because you will need the room for your food baby.

I've only been to Loveless for breakfast. This is partially because the rumors of their decadent breakfast were what first brought me in, and also because I live on the other side of town and have committed to living in a city without a car for at least year. West Nashville is (go figure) on other side of the city from my place in East Nashville. Here is the good news, unlike alcohol laws, there are no laws that dictate when you can start eating pie. Try to get over to Loveless during the week, as the weekend breakfast wait goes well into lunch.

29. CITY HOUSE SERVES PIZZA WITH SOUTHERN FLAIR

On Sunday's City House's Chef, Tandy Hilson, curates a Sunday Supper menu that highlights locally sourced ingredients. Those of us in the industry will always find out which Chefs have a tendency to occasionally provide a glimpse of their creative process. If you are able to visit City House on a Sunday, it is likely you are dining with some local chefs, servers, and restauranters lucky enough to have a Sunday off. When I first heard of the Sunday Suppers, I was told it was the Chef's research and development day. Say no more.

The menu at City House finds its foundation in traditional Italian cuisine that is artfully blended with Southern ingredients. At City House you will find all the requirements of quality Italian, the pizza dough is made from scratch and then aged for up to three days, the salami is made in house, the margherita sauce is balanced and exhibits layers of flavor developed over hours of simmering.

As with most of the restaurants on this list, City House only seeks out local ingredients for its menu. At City House that applies to its meats and its produce, which is led City House to be well-regarded for its sides, salads, and vegetable centric main dishes. The first few times I ate at City House, I noticed a pizza with a sunny side up egg on top of it, but I couldn't find it on the menu. Turns out, you can add it to any pizza. I would also ask for a fork and knife.

30. MAKE NEW FRIENDS AT REDHEADED STRANGER

It's no wonder I really enjoyed my experience at Redheaded Stranger. The chef whose brain made such an insightful menu, Michael Shemtov, is the chef who designed the first restaurant I fell in love with here in Nashville (Butcher & Bee, which of course made this list). I knew the whipped feta taco reminded me of something…aka the most popular appetizer at Butcher & Bee. Anyways, let's talk about Redheaded Stranger. Those of you who are music minded will recognize the homage to a Willie Nelson song (My dad picked up on it right away). We asked the server and were happy to find out that the Nelson family supported this act of adoration. Pretty cool.

Had I not been told that Chef Shemtov was behind Butcher & Bee as well I may not have realized it. The décor of Redheaded Stranger is on the complete other end of the spectrum. Butcher & Bee is dark and earthy, Redheaded Stranger is bright and stark. They also feature artwork from local artists, which is always a win in my book.

But Chef Shemtov doesn't do the design, he does the food, and upon close examination you can see his influence. The cuisine at Redheaded Stranger is Tex-Mex, but like Butcher & Bee (which is Mediterranean inspired) there is a strong sense of Southern style cooking and ingredients fused into the menu. They have a tater-tot taco and a brisket taco that are both out of this world and by no means Tex-Mex as most people imagine it. The brisket was my favorite, but this is one of those places where instead of making recommendations, I would encourage you to explore the menu. Find something you recognize, but still kind of don't, and order it.

31. INNOVATIVE ITALIAN AT FOLK

I have a weakness for restaurants like Folk. It isn't just the food, it's the whole idea. In general, I am always at home at restaurants whose décor is accented by wood and stone. When combined with the right use of plants and stark simplicity, restaurants like Folk become very relaxing and grounding. A great way to start your meal. Folk does one better by using windows to bring in natural light that highlight the rugged beauty of the bare brick walls as well as shines off of their white marble bar top. As you can tell, I really enjoyed the vibe at Folk well before I had even ordered.

The menu at Folk is rustic Italian and of course features locally sourced ingredients. The highlight of the menu offerings in my opinion are the pizzas. Talk about taking a simple, common dish and executing it flawlessly. I recently learned that the owner of Folk, Philip Krajeck, also owns Rolf & Daughters (which also made this list.). It's no surprise then that he knew the right formula for Nashville. Folk has a Southern charm about it, and the menu, while Italian, has the same feel as well. The food is comforting and simple, yet somehow still elegant and refined.

As far as menu recommendations go, my favorite dish is their Lamb Meatballs. My favorite pizza features fermented potato, spicy provolone, pancetta, and garlic. The fermented potato adds an interesting starchy complexity to the pizza and really shines with the pancetta. Don't be thrown if you're unfamiliar with some of the ingredients on the menu, the servers are very knowledgeable and can easily point you in the right direction. They also certainly know their wine, and Folk has a fantastic selection of revolving wine options.

32. SURF, TURF, AND SCOTCH AT THE SOUTHERN STEAK & OYSTER

In a magical world, where money falls from the sky, cholesterol is good for you, and beef production isn't ravaging the environment; I would eat at The Southern Steak & Oyster three nights a week. And I know this sounds crazy coming from a chef and foodie, but I would eat the same meal every time.

I would start with a single malt scotch (they have one of the best selections I've found in Nashville) paired with a dozen raw oysters (also some of the best in Nashville). Next, while finishing the scotch, I would have their New South Caesar salad. Arguably one of the most unique versions of the classic salad I have ever had that still preserves the essence of a good Caesar salad. For the main course I would switch over to a nice deep red, probably a Cab, and pair it with 'The Belle". That's the name for their Filet option. A juicy, grass-fed filet mignon topped with fried onions and a balsamic glaze. Served with asparagus, portabella shroomies, and their chived mashed potatoes. The final course would be one of their featured desserts (I'd switch it up here) and one of their many cordials or after dinner liquors (paired with the dessert of course).

Afterwards I would walk off the buzz and food coma by strolling around Downtown Nashville. It's hard not to be in a good mood after a meal like that, oh and the service at The Southern is top notch. Only making the experience that much more enjoyable.

33. ICE CREAM & MILKSHAKES FROM BOBBIE'S DAIRY DIP

Those who know me will likely be confused by the appearance of an ice cream place on this list. I realize it may be blasphemy to some, but I hate ice cream. If I wanted to put something frozen in my mouth I would just as soon eat snow. I am part of that one millionth of the population that is unable to comprehend why people like freezing their esophagus, but to each their own right. That being said, I don't have any idea how the ice cream at Bobbie's Dairy Dip tastes. I can tell you that nine out of every ten people I've seen there is eating ice cream. So, it must be good, and they certainly have a lot of options.

I went to Bobbie's for another reason. Growing up my Dad always sought out classic milkshake and burger places. Each one we discovered was compared to this mythical burger place he frequented growing up in Texas. I have not had the chance to take him to Bobbie's yet, but I am confident that it would please him (or anyone else who came to age here in the States during the mid 1900's.).

Bobbie's looks the part, and the food they put out hits the spot. They understand the value of hand-cut fries. They've not forgotten the lost art of brushing the burger bun with melted butter before placing it on the flattop, just long enough to crispen the edges. They also understand that a strawberry milkshake should actually have strawberries in it. Yes, I do enjoy milkshakes. They are cold, yes, but they are not frozen (although I tend to let them sit for a bit if they are too cold, or too thick.). Bobbie's strawberry milkshake was not too thick, or too cold. It was, like the fries and burger I had, a delicious representation of classic Americana cuisine. The experience of ordering through a small window and waiting to hear your name only adds to the fun.

34. PRINCE'S HOT CHICKEN IS A NASHVILLE ORIGINAL

Prince's Hot Chicken is one of two hot chicken places that made my list. I did recently learn that the one I choose to omit is the oldest, though maybe not the favorite. I discuss why I don't engage in hometown food wars when I introduce the other hot chicken spot.

Prince's appears to be the most well-funded of the three. I do believe there are multiple locations, maybe bordering on a chain. Nonetheless, just like when I went to Hattie B's, the line was insane. By this point, you're probably familiar with my view of lines. Lines are good. Patience is good. Being patient in long lines is rewarding. Waiting in line at Prince's will be rewarding. Repeat.

Their chicken was perfectly cooked, with a great crunch and tender inside. I did make the rookie mistake and ordered medium spice. Most of you will read this (and likely hear from others) and still decide to be brave, but either way I will still warn you. Medium heat and above at a hot chicken place is not a regulated heat scale. I love spicy food, but if it weren't for the incredible pickles and creamy coleslaw I ordered with my chicken, there is a chance I may not have made it. Cayenne is the principle bad guy in hot chicken, and cayenne is not a forgiving spice. You've been warned.

35. BEER AND BOWLING AT PINEWOOD SOCIAL

Pinewood Social can be a tad overwhelming when you first arrive. You may have thought you were going bowling, or to eat out, or to get a drink. But then you walk in and you realize you may be doing all of those things and more. I didn't count, but I am pretty sure there are at least a half dozen different things happening in there. The place is massive, and can seem chaotic, but they've done a good job organizing the chaos. I've heard of Pinewood Social described as a Dave & Busters for foodies and I'll admit that's probably the best way to describe the place.

Pinewood Social is meant to be a hangout and with a variety of ways to kill time, so it makes sense. Not surprisingly, I killed most of my time eating. I knew before I got there that the menu was designed to take traditional comfort foods and elevate them. Enter, a classic Rueben...with beef tongue. I realize tongue isn't the most popular part of the cow to eat, but I would bet that if you didn't know it was tongue, you would never know. (My editor is going to love that sentence). Some other notables on their menu, their pot roast, their fried broccoli starter, and my personal favorite chicken and waffles.

36. TWO TEN JACK IS NASHVILLE'S ACE FOR SUSHI

Two Ten Jack is arguably one of the best Japanese inspired restaurants I've ever been to. They took an interesting approach to the cuisine and the experience. Two Ten Jack feels more like a Japanese gastropub then it does your typically sushi house. The décor is a big contributor to that feeling. The design screams craft cocktails and chef driven food options. The kicker is how well the Japanese element is blended in. Props to the minds behind this one.

I have not had the chance to completely explore their entire menu yet, it's big. They have a lot of offerings but fortunately the menu is designed to taste. They have nearly twenty options for yakitori (skewers) and you order them one at a time. My favorite was the wagyu short rib skewer. A good amount of wagyu for a reasonable price, and of course delicious. Two Ten Jack also features a variety of creative sushi rolls, quality sashimi, some delicious ramen, an expansive small plates menu, and much more. Their cocktails mostly feature some form of sake or other Asian spirit, another example of the clever concept.

37. ADD TO YOUR HOT CHICKEN EXPERTISE AT HATTIE B'S

Hattie B's Hot Chicken is one of three Nashville hot chicken spots that people claim are the local originals. I have friends in Philly, and I have learned the hard way not to enter a hometown food war. I do not have the expertise to say who has been here the longest, who was first, or who is the best. I will say this, two of those places made this list, the one that didn't, just didn't do it for me. (I'll have my hate mail PO Box up and running before this gets published.)

Hattie B's made my list because it was really freaking good, and also really freaking spicy. Incorporating heat into the coating as opposed to a sauce is a simple change but one that really does make a difference. Word to wise though, unless you are the type to go Thai Hot++, start with a milder option. The key troublemaker is cayenne and cayenne does not care. That's what makes Nashville hot chicken unique.

My favorite thing to get at Hattie B's is only available on Sundays. It is a dish that hits every taste bud and texture receptor on our pallet. It is sweet, spicy, savory, doughy dish that is crispy, crunchy, airy, and moist. You may have guessed by now that I am talking about chicken and waffles. Hattie B's has one of the best versions I've had on this side of the Mississippi. The waffles are just the right size and consistency to serve as a warm yummy bed for the hot chicken. All of which is drenched, yes drenched, in syrup. You will have to wait in line for this experience, but it will be worth the wait I assure you.

38. CAMP, THE BAR FORMERLY KNOWN AS NO.308

Shortly after I arrived in Nashville, a bar some of my bartender friends highly recommended was planning on re-branding itself after over a decade of being one of Nashville's top spots for craft cocktails. A good friend of mine who has been a Nashville local for over twenty years say that No.308 was the cities original craft bar. Original or not, I got to stop in once while they were still No.308. The experience lived up to their reputation. The bartenders knew their craft and enjoyed making custom cocktails for patrons. I had high hopes for CAMP (the new name for the bar formerly known as No.308).

The idea behind CAMP was to pay homage to our national parks. The interior décor has a camping feel and both times I've been there I have witness people getting their drink on while getting their arts and craft on as well. They say adult beverages can support creativity; I dig it. Their new cocktails also fall in line with the theme. For example, they have an Everglades cocktail that features tequila, orange, lemon, and guava. While I don't typically go for the mixed drinks, I actually tried a few here. I wasn't disappointed and got to sleep better at night knowing that some of the proceeds get donated to the national parks.

Oh yeh, they also have oysters and caviar. I didn't try the caviar, but I had a few oysters and can attest to their quality. Another fun thing about CAMP, they have a tableside s'mores dessert. It paired wonderfully with their Glacier cocktail.

39. GET CARBON NEUTRAL COFFEE AT CREMA

Crafting a list this long (even in a city full of options like Nashville) makes it difficult to avoid repeating genres/cuisine types. I've tried to take steps to avoid only mentioning places that offer cuisines I prefer, and I set a limit on how many coffee shops I would allow to make the cut. I've also tried to separate similar concepts within the list. Lastly, when I've included similar places, I have made sure to highlight what makes those places different from the others.

Crema is a coffee shop and roaster located in Downtown Nashville. They have all the things that one would want in a good coffee shop, great beans, knowledgeable and skilled baristas, and a few delicious small bites. The décor at crema is more in line with the stark, open, and bright style versus the cozy bookworm style. Crema also takes their coffee seriously. They've won quite a few awards for the specialty roasts and that expertise is clear even in the simplest of items (my double espresso, for example, had a silky and delicate crema and was just the right

temperature to bring out all of the flavor notes.).
While I was there, I noticed the baristas constantly
monitoring the settings on the machine, mindful of
how subtle changes can really impact the quality of
the pull.

There is another aspect of Crema that differentiates
them from some of the other top notch coffee shops in
town. The back-story and business philosophy of
Crema illustrates that their diligence and caring
approach goes past the quality of their roast. The
owners of Crema started with a less than ideal amount
of capital (something I know all too well). This means
that in addition to designing the normal aspects of
their new business venture, they were also painting,
sanding, building, decorating, etc. I opened my first
café like this, and I am only envious that at the very
least the owners of Crema probably had unlimited
access to coffee for most of it. That aspect of Crema's
backstory is admirable and commendable, but the
thing that really stood out to me was their approach to
sustainability. They are carbon neutral, which is no
small feat for a coffee shop that does its own roasting.
They've also chosen to take responsibility for the
farmers they source their coffee from by paying fair
prices and employing ethical business practices (this

may not seem like a big deal but look up the ethics of the global coffee trade sometime, you will see what I mean.).

If the quality of the coffee at Crema isn't enough to convince you to stop by, hopefully the stance they've taken on increasing the quality of the global experience will.

40. COZY UP AT THE PATTERSON HOUSE

The Patterson House was another unexpected find for me when I first moved to Nashville. I was looking for a unique brunch place and had a friend visiting me who at the time owned a craft cocktail bar. She had heard of The Patterson House from another mixologist friend and so we ventured out to check it out. Walking in, we both knew we were in for a treat. The word cozy doesn't do justice for The Patterson House, the menu was clearly chef driven, and the cocktails were bound to be well crafted. There had to have been at least three hundred different spirits on that bar.

I'm not much of a mixed drink guy, I prefer to try different scotches and other spirits either neat or with a dash of cold water. Both my friend and I had zero chance of making it through all the spirit offerings at The Patterson House. We tried our best, and brunch quickly turned into a late lunch. The bartenders were excited to see how adventurous we were, and after trying most of the cocktails on the menu, they started introducing me to spirits I'd never heard of while making their own creative drinks for my friend.

I want to make sure to give a nod towards their menu as well. It was in a lot of ways similar to their cocktail menu. Traditional favorites made with high quality ingredients and a few unique spins just to add some personal flair to the experience. Some notable options were their smoked wings, served with a white BBQ sauce, and their coconut napoleon dessert.

41. CARNICERIA SAN LUIS IS MORE THAN A BUTCHER SHOP

Carniceria San Luis is located in Downtown Nashville on 4th avenue. It is among several other places offering international cuisine. The evening I discovered it, I was walking back home from dinner and decided to take a longer route to digest and check out more of downtown. Despite being very full (I don't remember where I ate beforehand), the smell of roasting meat and the aromatic aroma of caramelized onions left me no other choice but to find its source. I detected the Latin essence to the aroma and up until this point had not been able to find authentic Mexican food in Nashville. (I think I had only lived in the city a few months at this point.)

Walking into the Carniceria was like a quick trip back home, or better yet abroad (Miami has more Cuban influence than Mexican influence.). You are greeted by counters of select cuts of meat, whole smoked chickens, tamales, a variety of salsas, fresh juices, and much more. Carniceria San Luis is first and foremost a butcher and a market, but like most international markets it offered an extensive menu of hot and ready to eat food. I ordered a whole smoked chicken and started nibbling little pieces off here and there as I walked back home. A mile later, and it looked like a bird of prey had gotten a hold of the thing (and I had just ate a full meal, you know the one I was supposed to be walking off).

42. CELEBRATE THE HIGHLIFE AT BASTION

Bastion is one of the few Nashville restaurants that I was informed of well before I moved to town. Two good chef friends of mine were doing a honeymoon food tour/road trip back in 2017 and Bastion was among several places they stopped at that resulted in me receiving a barrage of food porn images.

Bastion's classification is that of a chef's table dining experience. There is an open kitchen that provides a constant view of the art being created. You can get even closer to the action by dining at the bar top directly in front of the chefs. True to their chef roots, the menu at Bastion is constantly changing. You are actually greeted by a paper print out of what they have available that day and a pen to make you selections. Once you make your selections, the chefs take charge, and you sit back and relax.

Everything I ate was incredibly beautiful to look at and full of flavors artfully crafted with the same skill and precision as the plating. I ended up ordering at least six courses and got to enjoy several delicacies, including oysters, squab, and beef tartare. An added bonus, the back bar at Bastion features several classic spirits that are quite rare. If you are an adventurous eater and drinker, I would highly encourage you to pair your meal with some of their unique spirits.

43. BROWN'S DINER FOR A CLASSIC DINER EXPERIENCE

Sometimes you want a cheeseburger. Not just any cheeseburger though, there are the gourmet ones, the yummy grease laden bar food ones, and then there is the classic diner style cheeseburger served at Brown's. You will notice I didn't mention fast food, that's because (sorry not sorry) fast food is anything but food. Come change my mind. We can meet at Brown's and I will try to listen while I drift in and out of memories I don't even have because I was born in the 80's, as I munch on their cheeseburger.

Brown's approach to diner food is to keep it simple and keep it classic. It is unlikely any of their recipes have changed since it opened in the late 1920's. The flattop is well worn in, and you can taste it when you bite into that cheeseburger. I wasn't around in the early 1900's but if this what cheeseburgers started as, it's hard to understand the evolutionary turn we took to get to big whooper mac town.

44. THERE IS ALWAYS SOMETHING TO LOOK FORWARD TO THE OPTIMIST

I was optimistic about The Optimist when I looked up their menu and noticed they were a purist seafood house. They had maybe two or three items on the menu that didn't feature seafood. I realize it may seem limiting but when a restaurant commits to being so specific, trust them.

The Optimist's menu takes in a variety of fish and shellfish from around the world and then pairs them with elegant southern recipes. They feature a variety of oysters and I usually order two of each variety so I can sample them all. Their cocktail menu also stood out to me. I really only drink scotch or wine when I dine out, but I often sit at the bar. At The Optimist, I got to try a few of the cocktails, and they were well crafted. The service was The Optimist was also notable.

45. SPOOKY GOOD FOOD AT SKULL'S RAINBOW ROOM

If I were to tell you, "Hey I am going to take you this great prime rib place that also has a burlesque show." You would probably be intrigued, if not confused. Then we would walk down Printer's Alley, in the heart of touristy Downtown Nashville. You would see neon lit bars and most likely a slew of people at varied levels of intoxication shuffling between the several bars in the alley. One of those neon signs would be for Skull's Rainbow Room and as we got closer and you realized where we were going for prime rib, you'd probably begin to doubt my judgement.

Well don't. I was equally apprehensive when I was first told to visit Skulls. I remember looking at my phone's map app and determining where it was located and politely telling whoever it was that recommended the place how much I loath tourist places. I can also count the amount of country songs I like on one hand. Then I saw an article that talked about the history of Skull's Rainbow Room.

Skull's Rainbow Room first opened in 1948 and was the haunt of the likes of Johnny Cash, in a time where Printer's Alley was as known for gambling, drunken debauchery, and womanizing as it was known for having printing presses. The Skull's that exists today is version two of the original Skull's, but the vibe is still very much the same. It's mostly the menu that has changed (the old menu is displayed on the walls, along with other memorabilia for the old days).

I was told to try the Prime Rib. I will tell you to try the Prime Rib. I strongly encourage you to try the Prime Rib. Have I mentioned that their Prime Rib is worth trying?

46. A STEAK AND A BREW FROM 12 SOUTH TAPROOM & GRILL

Before living in Nashville, I lived in Tampa, FL. Between Tampa and the neighboring city of St. Petersburg, there are a ton of beer halls/breweries. A lot of them are pretty well known nationally. I spent considerable time when I lived there trying all of them in search of the standouts. When I arrived in Nashville and saw how many options there were and I decided to take a different approach. I started asking people who I met at other restaurants and eateries which ones were their favorites. It started as a long list, but the tallies mounted next to the common mentions, and 12 South Taproom & Grill was among a few that started to take a commanding lead. Satisfied with my polling efforts, I decided to check it out (there would be no need for a recount).

Before I even gazed upon the beer or food menu, I was already understanding the appeal. The décor is eclectic and vibrant, and the giant chalkboard full of beer options implies they change the list often. I don't know beer like I know wine and scotch, so I explained to the bartender my preferences and let her take the reins.

Thus, began a guided journey of beer tasting that I think ended with my trying at least a dozen options (not even putting a dent in the total options.). Between the vibe, the food, and the service, I lost track of which ones were my favorite but was comforted by the reminder that it didn't matter, they may all have been rotated out by the next time I visit.

The food offerings weren't extraordinarily unique, the menu has a variety of common gastropub options. But this was by no means a bad thing, sometimes you just want some brisket blanketed nachos, or scratch made potato wedges. The trick is knowing which bar gets them right. The chef who designed this menu got them right. I started with the aforementioned brisket nachos and finished it off with their Groovin Reuben.

47. LOCKELAND TABLE FOR CLASSIC ITALIAN FAIR WITH A SOUTHERN FLAIR

I found Lockeland Table on accident. I was walking around my East Nashville neighborhood one night, like actually in the neighborhood. I take walks often and I try to switch it up, it's cool to see the type of homes in different areas. This night I was walking down Woodland St. I usually wander down streets a little further from Main but I noticed that Woodland suddenly veered away from Main and decided to follow it. A few blocks in, bam, I am standing in front of Lockeland Table. It looks like it could be someone's home, but is clearly an eatery, so I strolled on in. The food gods from every culture since the Aztecs must have been looking out for me that day.

The menu at Lockeland Table is Italian-American fusion but also had some Hispanic elements to it (There was empanadas and tacos on the menu.). Like most of the places I have chosen for this list they take great care to use local ingredients. Those ingredients force a slight nod towards Southern cuisine, which really elevates their offerings. They have a salad, for example, that features fried green tomatoes and a local jam that was topped with just the right amount of this bleu cheese dressing that had these smokey hints to it. It was a great version of a classic dish. They also have a dessert, that may be one of the best things I have ever eaten. It combines two of my favorite classic desserts, banana foster and bread pudding. Do I need to say anything else? How about its topped with a rum infused cremé anglaise? I'm sure they are used to people ordering that first, I may start there next time.

48. OLD SCHOOL COFFEE FEELS FROM THE DRUG STORE

Yes, I know, another coffee shop. This is the last one I promise. I have tried to not only choose coffee shops that have a quality brew and tasty supporting baked goods, but to also make sure all of the ones on this list have been unique. As a writer (and coffee fiend) I spend a lot of time in coffee shops and as weird as it may sound, I choose which one to go to based on what I will be writing that day. Surviving as an entry-level freelance writer means you have to be willing and able to write anything. So, it helps to have places that support different vibes.

As you may have gathered from the name, The Drug Store is reminiscent of early 20th century soda and coffee bars. Located on the ground floor of the Hotel Noelle, The Drug Store was at one point, actually a drug store. Now it is one of a few great food destinations at the Hotel Noelle. You will find skilled baristas, great roast options, and some very scrumptious baked goods. All delivered in the type of coffee shop atmosphere that makes you want to sit and read the daily papers while watching pedestrians stroll the streets of Downtown Nashville. This isn't just a run of the mill hotel coffee shop.

49. BLUEGRASS AT THE STATION INN

I am pretty sure that at one point in this list I shared how little I like Country Music. If I am being brutally honest, despise is probably the best way to describe my sentiments for that music genre. That being said, there is still something to be said for live music. Station Inn, which is in the Gulch, is hailed as one of the last traditional music venues here in Nashville. I've been there a few times and every time the music being played was described to me as 'Bluegrass', not Country. So, update, I like Bluegrass. It has some of the same sounds as Country music, minus the whining and repetitive melody.

Another great thing about the Station Inn is that they've got a limited but really decent grub menu and an extensive beer selection. This is more of a stop in during the evening and have a few drinks while listening to (surprisingly) good music type of place. I typically order something to munch on, and if you're looking for a good option to go with the mood, I recommend the pimento cheese tray.

50. MARGOT CAFÉ IS THE HOME OF FRENCH CUISINE IN NASHVILLE

Margot Café is in East Nashville (my stomping grounds), an area of Nashville I would argue hosts the most eclectic variety of people and eateries. My dad says it's the most hipster area, but I am waiting for that term to be a bit more flushed out before I add it to my lexicon (Mostly because I have been called a hipster and a millennial before and while I may be both of those things I am going to resist being labeled because it's the right thing to do as a millennial anti-establishment hipster foodie.).

Margot's Café is owned and operated by Margot McCormack, a Nashville native who honed her culinary skills in the great culinary pantheon that is NY City. She opened her café with the desire to source only local Tennessee products for her

Southern French inspired menu. Margot's Café is hailed as one of the first restaurants to brave the risks of East Nashville twenty years ago. I was not in Nashville yet but living here now I can see how the areas storied grit has led to its charm. As a city folk, I love it.

These days, Margot's Café is an institution in East Nashville. It's got a cozy and romantic feel to it. The menu changes daily, so I can't give you any recommendations. I can just tell you I have yet to be disappointed.

READ OTHER BOOKS BY
CZYK PUBLISHING

Eat Like a Local United States Cities & Towns

Eat Like a Local United States

Eat Like a Local- Oklahoma: Oklahoma Food Guide

Eat Like a Local- North Carolina: North Carolina Food Guide

Eat Like a Local- New York City: New York City Food Guide

Children's Book: Charlie the Cavalier Travels the World by Lisa Rusczyk

EAT LIKE A LOCAL

Follow *Eat Like a Local on* Amazon.
Join our mailing list for new books

http://bit.ly/EatLikeaLocalbooks

CZYKPublishing.com